LOVE YOU
MY
BABY GIRL

This Book Belongs To:

"No matter how old my daughter gets,
she'll always be my baby girl"

Date:...../..../........

"You are the beautiful gift that i receive every day. My life is so magical because of you, my dearest little girl"

Date:...../..../........

"Dresses are just a picture of how much we want
to decorated as women but there's no better
decoration than a mother's love for her daughter"

Date:..../..../........

Date:..../..../........

"There will be so many times you feel like you've failed but in the Eyes, Heart, and Mind of your child you are super mom"

Date:...../..../........

Date:...../..../........

I only miss you when i'm breathing

Date:..../..../........

"How is it possible that out of all the little girls
in the whole world we got the best ones"

Date:..../..../........

"You'll be; her first kiss, her first love, her first friend. You are her mommy & she is your whole world. She is your baby girl"

Date:...../..../........

Date:...../..../........

"A prayer for my daughter, Dear God, your gifts are many. I'm grateful! for every one. One of the greatest gift you've given IS THE GIFT OF MY DEAR DAUGHTER. Thanks for her life dear lord"

Date:...../..../........

Date:..../..../........

"And I promise you this; no matter who enters
your life, I will love you more than any of them"

Date:...../..../........

Date:..../..../........

"I want you to believe deep in your heart that
you are capable of achieving anything you put
your mind to, That you will Never Lose"

Date:...../..../........

Date:..../..../........

"There has never been, nor will there ever be,
anything quite so special "as the love" between
the mother and a daughter"

Date:...../..../........

Having a daughter is like creating a replica of yourself, you think you are cranky and moody? wait till she arrives and gives you double for the trouble

Date:..../..../........

Date:...../..../........

"As your mother i promise you that i will always be in
one of three places; in front of you to cheer you on,
behind you to have your back, or next to you so that
you aren't alone"

Date:...../..../........

"Never forget that i love you life is filled with good
times and hard times. Learn from everything you can,
Be the Great woman I know you can be"

Date:...../..../........

Date:...../...../........

"You will forever be my always"

Date:..../..../........

"The love between mom and her girl
is unbreakable"

Date:...../..../........

Date:...../...../........

"My daughter is Super Amazing and i'm
the lucky one because i get to be her mom"

Date:...../..../........

"A daughter is god's way of saying,
Thought you could use a lifelong friend"

Date:..../..../........

"And she loved a little girl very, very much, even more than she loved herself"

Date:...../..../........

"The bond between mother and
daughter lasts a lifetime"

Date:...../..../........

"A daughter is a gift of love"

Date:..../..../........

"Mother's love is peace. It need not be acquired it need not be deserved"

Date:...../...../........

Date:...../...../........

"You are my daughter, my moon my stars"

Date:...../..../........

"Mother is her daughter's first god. She must teach her the most important lesson of all—
how to love"

Date:..../..../........

"Mothers are inscrutable beings to
their daughters always"

Date:...../..../........

"You make me so proud to be your mother,
and i hope that I make you proud to be my
daughter, too.... I love you"

Date:...../..../........

> "No one else will ever know the strength of my love
> for you. After all you're the only one who knows
> what my heart sounds like from the inside"

Date:..../..../........

"A mother's arms are made of tenderness
and children sleep soundly in them"

Date:...../..../........

"A mother is she who can take the place of all others, but whose place no one else can take"

Date:..../..../........

Date:...../...../........

"So there's this girl. She kinda stole my
heart. She calls me 'mom"

Date:..../..../........

Date:..../..../........

"My daughter is my baby, today, tomorrow, and always. You hurt her, I will hurt you. I don't care if she's 1 day or 50 years old, I will defend and protect her all of my life"

Date:...../..../........

Date:..../..../........

"To my dearest daughter, I want you to know that forever you will be in my heart no matter the distance. I love you"

Date:...../...../........

Date:...../...../........

"Stay close to people who feel like sunshine"

Date:...../...../........

Date:...../..../........

"Her little hand stole my heart and her
little feet ran away with it"

Date:..../..../........

Date:...../...../........

"I will always be your number one supporter
for i care for you the most in this life of ours"

Date:...../..../........

"Love your mother, the most beautiful person
on this earth. Our best critic, yet our
strongest supporter"

Date:...../..../........

Date:...../...../........

"No matter how busy a person's day may be,
If they really care, they will always find time
for you"

Date:...../...../........

Date:..../..../........

"Your daughter will hold your hand only for
a little while. But she will hold your heart for
a lifetime"

Date:..../..../........

"I know a girl, She puts the color
inside of my world"

Date:..../..../........

Date:...../...../........

"My daughter is my heart and everything"

Date:..../..../........

"A mom's treasure is her daughter,
Always and forever."

Date:...../..../........

"Daughters may grow into women and grow out of their toys, but in the hearts of others they are still their little girls"

Date:..../..../........

"Sometimes when i need a miracle i look into
eyes of my child and realize i already have one"

Date:...../...../........

Date:...../...../........

"Daughter, You outgrew my lap, but
never my heart"

Date:...../..../........

Date:...../..../........

"When they placed you in my arms, You
slipped into my heart"

Date:...../..../........

"I can't promise to fix all your problems but i
can promise you won't have to face them all
alone"

Date:...../..../.......

Date:...../...../.......

"A mother is the first love of her
daughter, and a daughter is a whole world
for a mother"

Date:...../..../........

Date:...../...../........

"Always love your mother because you
will never get another"

Date:..../..../........

Date:...../..../........

"My daughter is awesome and i am the
luckiest one because i get to be her mother"

Date:..../..../........

"Children are the anchors of a
mother's life"

Date:...../...../........

Date:...../...../........

"Thank heaven for little girl"

Date:...../..../........

Date:...../...../........

"A daughter is one of the most beautiful
gifts this world has to give"

Date:...../..../........

Date:..../..../........

"The best thing about having you as a mom
is my kids having you as a grandma"

Date:...../..../........

"No matter what life throws at me at
least i don't have ugly children"

Date:..../..../........

Date:...../...../........

"We won't need to give a birthday present.
We already made you the perfect gift.... our
daughter"

Date:...../..../........

"A child's laugh could simply be one of
the most beautiful sounds in the world"

Date:..../..../........

"To my children.. If i had choose between loving you and breathing.. I would use my last breath to tell you... I Love You"

Date:...../...../........

Date:..../..../........

"I may not have it together everyday, but
we are together everyday and that's all that
matters"

Date:...../..../........

Date:...../..../........

"I am your mom it's not my job to give you what you want.. It's my job to show you what you need and help you learn how to get those things for yourself"

Date:...../..../........

"You're not just my daughter you are my reason for living the love of my life, and the queen of my heart. I love you, My dearest daughter!"

Date:...../..../.......